Shadows & Light

Shadows & Light: Haiku/Senryū

by Laughton J. Collins, Jr.

Shadows & Light: Haiku/Senryū Copyright © 2024 Laughton J. Collins, Jr.

Published by Requiem Press.

All rights reserved. No part of this publication may be reproduced or transmitted in any form or by any means, electronic or mechanical, including photocopy, recording, or any information storage and retrieval system, without permission in writing from the publisher.

https://requiempress.weebly.com/
https://laughtoncollinsjr.com/

Cover art Copyright © 2024 Melissa C. Gumms

A Requiem Press Book

ISBN: 979-8-9899561-5-9

All go unto one place; all are of the dust, and all turn to dust again. (**Ecclesiastes 3:20**)

The fool foldeth his hands together, and eateth his own flesh. (**Ecclesiastes 4:5**)

Introduction

Haiku are a traditional form of Japanese short poetry. They are written in 3 lines containing a syllabic count of 5/7/5. The haiku are poems about nature and contain a kireji or "cutting word" and a kigo or "season word." Senryū are similar to haiku in structure but don't follow the other rules applied to the haiku. Rather than being about nature, Senryū are short poems about human nature, written in the 5/7/5 syllabic format but without the "cutting word" or "season word." Haiku and senryū do not usually rhyme but they can. There is no law and/or rule against rhyming haiku and/or senryū, it's just not generally done.

Senryū are named after the Japanese poet Karai Senryū who said, "enough with these haiku all serious about nature, no one cares about that." So he wrote his own poems in a similar style to haiku and everyone else was like, "Well, these obviously aren't haiku. We'd look like foolish Americans if we call them haiku." So someone suggested calling them 'poems of the river willow' and someone smarter said, "Why don't we just call them senryū?" So the name senryū stuck and that's what they are known as today, except in America where they are almost always just called haiku. That is all almost certainly not true as I just made it up but Karai Senryū is the namesake of the poem that bears his name.

There is rarely a distinction made between haiku and senryū in English poetry. Most of the haiku written in English are actually senryū. The two forms have been merged. Also, there are virtually no rules to writing haiku in English. There's no need for a cutting word, a season word or a 3 line limit, the 5/7/5 syllabic structure is not adhered to and haiku that do not follow these rules are preferred in most cases by most people but not me.

The poems in this book might actually be best described as haiku/senryū adjacent poems. They look like they might be haiku/senryū. They follow the 3 lines with 5/7/5 syllabic structure but probably don't contain a "cutting word" or a "season word," which would be fine if they are senryū. They are not always about nature or human nature, some are about god and satan and other not real supernatural imaginary things. None of the haiku I've written contain a "cutting word," mainly because I don't know what that is. If any of my haiku contain a "cutting word," it's completely by accident and unintentional. All of my haiku/senryū adjacent poems follow the 3 lines with 5/7/5 syllabic structure because that's pretty much the definition of both haiku and senryū. And, I find the constraint of the syllabic structure to be more of a challenge. It would be much easier to write haiku and/or senryū if you do not have to fit your thoughts and/or ideas into 3 lines of 5/7/5 syllables.

     Maybe none of this is true. Maybe none of this matters. Maybe this was just me wasting your time on nonsense before you read the nonsense that follows. I hope you enjoy the nonsense of these haiku/senryū adjacent poems.

Laughton J. Collins, Jr.

The following Haiku/Senryū adjacent poems were first published in Runaway Train of Thought

VI - in autumns' moonlight
CXIX - baptism by fire
CXX - if love were a war
CXXI - now i'm just a ghost
CXXII - losing the battle
CXXIII - my heart is broken—

The following Haiku/Senryū adjacent poem was also published in They're Gonna Crucify Me

CXIX - baptism by fire

I

we stand in darkness
our lives illuminate
in shadows and light—

II

a voice in my head
cracking my brain like thunder
sounds like god to me—

All religions are founded on the fear of the many
and the cleverness of the few. — Stendhal

III

god's face in the sky
burns violently, mid-day
resurrected sun—

IV

love is a demon
consuming everything
in my heart shaped box—

If there is a God, he is a malign thug. – Mark Twain

V

life and death collide
love and hate interject pain
but i carry on—

VI

in autumns' moonlight
stars prick holes into the sky
but nothing gets through—

Poetry is a mirror which makes beautiful that which is distorted. — Percy Bysshe Shelley

VII

she fucking hates me
because of the way my heart
beat her heart to death—

VIII

i am not dead yet
i have so much life to live
and dreams unfulfilled—

IX

the first day of spring
my mind wanders back to you
and our last spring—

X

in pornography
the body is a weapon
daggers piercing flesh—

XI

today is tonight
tomorrow is tomorrow
where is yesterday—?

XII

another easter
has come resurrecting me
from the death of sleep—

XIII

years are passing by
time's moving much faster now
we've all gotten old—

XIV

there is an echo
in the caverns of my chest
from my beating heart—

XV

on lake washington
rocks skipping on the surface
sink to the bottom—

XVI

another morning
resurrecting me again
from the death of sleep—

XVII

two butterflies dance
to their own butterfly tune
on a day in june—

XVIII

cigarette burning
ashes falling to the ground
smoke gets in my eyes—

XIX

look into my eyes
my eyes looking back at you
but now you have gone—

XX

the path of the wind
lake washington's morning breeze
the surface shimmers—

XXI

spring, autumn, winter
but what about the summer
we were together—?

XXII

sometimes life is kind
but death is often kinder
more peaceful, silent—

XXIII

the darkness of night
covers me like a blanket
wrapped tightly in sin—

XXIV

the devil in me
is trying even harder
to free himself now—

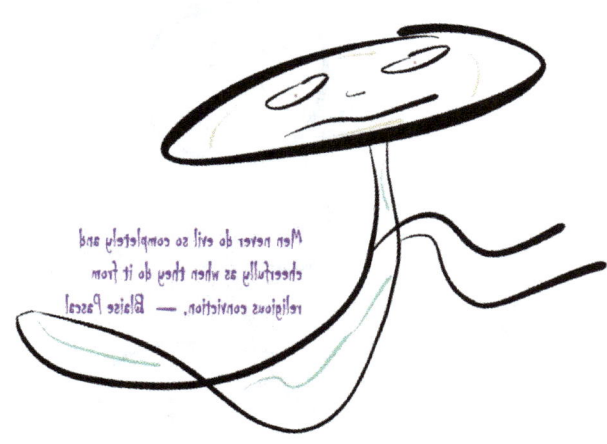

Men never do evil so completely and cheerfully as when they do it from religious conviction. — Blaise Pascal

XXV

the devil's my friend
he comforts me in this hell
this is my home now—

XXVI

jesus and his whore
keep crosses above their bed
their hearts crucified—

If God has spoken, why is the world not convinced. — Percy Bysshe Shelley

XXVII

heaven and hell are
two sides of a single coin
waiting to be flipped—

XXVIII

today's a new day
the sun screaming in the sky
so high above us—

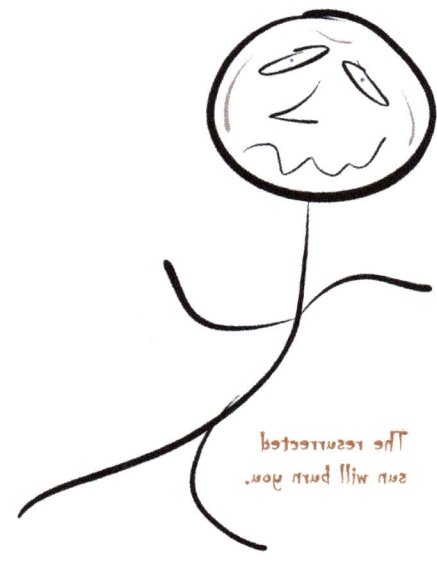

XXIX

yesterday i fell
from my place in the night sky
now i have no home—

XXX

when i see this road
life has streched out before me
i close my eyes tight—

We would be 1,500 years ahead if it hadn't been for the church dragging science back by its coattails and burning our best minds at the stake. — Catherine Fahringer

XXXI

mary magdalene
or the whore of babylon
satisfy the christ—

XXXII

silently i wept
with tears flowing silent rage
my heart exploded—

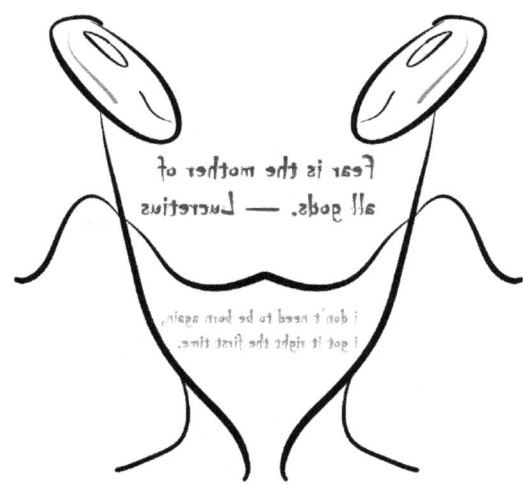

XXXIII

this demon i see
it's my mirrored reflection
looking back at me—

XXXIV

my heart is shattered
love is fractured, love bleeds out
i can't rebuild it—

XXXV

sometimes i can't breathe
there's too much space between us
too much————between us—

XXXVI

my heart is broken
into a million pieces
a jigsaw puzzle—

XXXVII

my life has ended
my death is just beginning
heaven and hell merged—

XXXVIII

stars fall from the sky
plummeting so fast—so slow
destruction follows—

XXXIX

life is a movie
love is an intermission
and death is the end—

XL

love is the chorus
to the battle hymn of hearts
but always off key—

XLI

god and/or his son
raised from the dead and/or life
heaven and/or hell—

XLII

love is a rocket
crash landed in the crater
of my broken heart—

If God really existed, it would be necessary
to abolish Him. — Mikhail Bakunin

XLIII

the greener the grass
the lonelier the field seems
with no cows to roam—

XLIV

darkness all around
no more sunny days ahead
night conquers the day—

The Christian god is a being of terrific character - cruel, vindictive, capricious and unjust. — Thomas Jefferson

XLV

a tree standing tall
nature's tower of babel
reaches for heaven—

XLVI

two butterflies dance—
to their own butterfly tune
on a windy day—

As long as you live, keep learning how to live. — Lucius Annaeus Seneca

XLVII

a total eclipse
has darkened the mid-day sky
god has closed his eyes—

XLVIII

god sits in heaven
planning his next genocide
but he sits alone—

Is God willing to prevent evil, but not able? Then he is not omnipotent. Is he able, but not willing? Then he is malevolent. Is he both able and willing? Then whence cometh evil? Is he neither able nor willing? Then why call him God? — Epicurus

XLIX

satan in disguise
climbing heaven's holy peak
god is defeated—

L

heaven lost its light
god sent the darkness to earth
pearly gates are closed—

Is man merely a mistake of God's? Or God merely
a mistake of man? — Friedrich Nietzsche

LI

in space there's no sound
god whispers his commandments
his voice like thunder—

LII

god is defeated
angels revolted again
their master dethroned—

god is a paradox

LIII

love leaves no traces
on the broken hearted few
or the ones like me—

LIV

angels in heaven
and humanity on earth
demons down below—

LV

explosions in space
a universe expanding
a galaxy born—

LVI

time is standing still
but we move so fast through space
no one notices—

LVII

in the sky above—
no god exists—no satan
in the hell below—

LVIII

i could never see
what wasn't in front of me
the past left behind—

there is no god

LIX

thunderstorms outside
crying thunderous applause
for the day that was—

LX

this is a haiku
here are seven syllables
and here are five more—

LXI

yesterday is gone
tomorrow has yet to come
today's all we have—

LXII

crucified again
on the cross above my bed
always wake up dead—

LXIII

i'm living in hell
the flames surround me again
extinguish the blaze—

LXIV

another sunrise
another morning glory
just another day—

heaven is an illusion

LXV

two conflicting views
of heaven and hell collide
the rapture's begun—

LXVI

reading the bible
creation—violence—death—
god is the villain—

LXVII

the war is over
the enemy is destroyed
but nothing has changed—

LXVIII

you entered the room
i became invisible
you never noticed—

LXIX

the sky is still blue
the sun still burns overhead
god kills us slowly—

LXX

lightning cracks the sky
the voice of god can be heard
in silent whispers—

LXXI

in stillness we find
god whispers in every breeze
life's eternal flame—

LXXII

love—a symphony
endless melodies emerge,
two souls harmonize—

LXXIII

another easter—
i'm resurrected again
from dying in sleep—

LXXIV

beneath the dark sky
calvary's hill stands silent
now—jesus is dead—

LXXV

a dying god-man
offers salvation from sin
but he's a liar—

LXXVI

messiah or christ—
the title doesn't matter
his name is crossed out—

LXXVII

last night i saw you
another dream or nightmare
vaguely familiar—

LXXVIII

the war is over—
i've been defeated again
my heart aches for you—

LXXIX

my chest is empty
that's where my heart used to be
before i met you—

LXXX

now my heart's broken
my love has no place to live
no shelter—no home—

LXXXI

life and death evolve
into an eternity
of heaven and hell—

LXXXII

no one can hear you
your words dancing in the air
the waltz—the tango—

LXXXIII

sacrificial lamb
left hanging upon your cross
the king of no one—

LXXXIV

space—a solitude
mysteries linger—untold
endless—vast unknown—

LXXXV

heaven's reflection
on the darkness of my soul
god has turned away—

LXXXVI

the sun is shining
the night has faltered again
just another day—

LXXXVII

in eternal light
heaven's reflection avoids
eternal darkness

LXXXVIII

my mind is scary
when i'm alone with my thoughts
keep me company—

A thousand Dreams within me
softly burn. — Arthur Rimbaud

LXXXIX

the sun is setting
darkness will overtake us
the sun will return—

XC

the sun disappeared
ran away from the darkness
but will rise again—

XCI

stars fall and stars die
sitting alone in darkness
they no longer shine—

XCII

souls locked in a war
good and evil existing
a battle within—

XCIII

a god-man dying
there never was salvation
hanging on his tree—

XCIV

i'm going to hell
that's where all the good times are
that's where you'll find me—

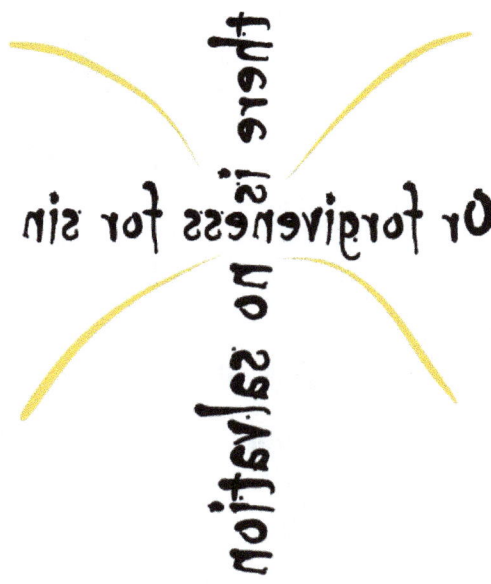

XCV

nature is a beast
setting the night on fire
volcanoes erupt—

XCVI

my heart skipped a beat
your name echoed through my chest
now love has found me—

XCVII

lost found lost again~
will you ever find me here?
lost in this black hole—

XCVIII

here i stand again
looking at mortality
through my tortured eyes—

XCIX

ivy covered trees
and rain falling silently
we walk in the park—

C

five seven and five
the syllables of each line
making a haiku—

CI

i'll never love you
any more than i do now
but i'll always try—

CII

like a razor blade
pressed firmly against my flesh
the wind cuts through me—

CIII

jesus never could
carry his own cross up hill
how could he bear mine—?

CIV

god is a drifter
without a heaven above
no place to call home—

CV

god is a demon
hiding beneath ancient skies
heaven's illusion—

CVI

we disappoint god
god disappoints creation
we had it coming—

god is the christian's
imaginary friend—
satan is their
imaginary enemy—

CVII

sitting in heaven
god creates disappointment
spreads it evenly—

CVIII

recycle your words
they no longer have meaning
now that i've moved on—

CIX

here we go again
setting the night on fire
just the two of us—

CX

i'm dreaming of you
but you are just the nightmare
i see every night—

Praying is talking to yourself in the dark when no one is listening. Praying is what the god fearing Christians do.

CXI

my heart has faded
my soul disappeared again
i'm lost without you—

CXII

the sun says goodnight
falls asleep in darkened skies
but rises again—

CXIII

internal anger
heart and soul explode sorrow
but life rages on—

CXIV

a christ crucified
sacrificed and sanctified
there's no salvation—

CXV

my nightmare's ended
and all of my dreams destroyed
you'll be back again—

CXVI

hearts that are broken
leave scars that can not be seen
the wounds never heal—

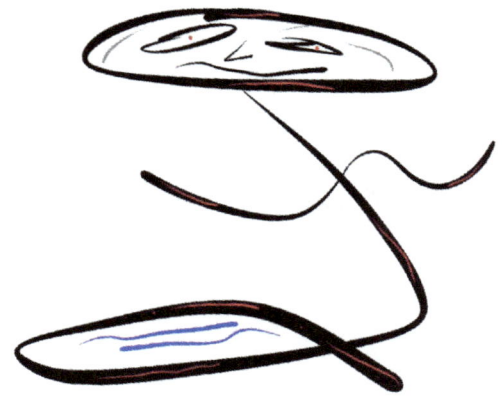

CXVII

a wooden cross stands
where many others have died
son of god destroyed—

CXVIII

every single day
the sun sits high in the sky
looking down on us—

god creates confusion

CXIX

baptism by fire
burning my soul and my skin
resurrecting me—

CXX

if love were a war
you would be victorious
and i defeated—

this is just a reflection

CXXI

now i'm just a ghost
of the man i used to be
you can see through me—

CXXII

losing the battle
in order to win the war
this is how we love—

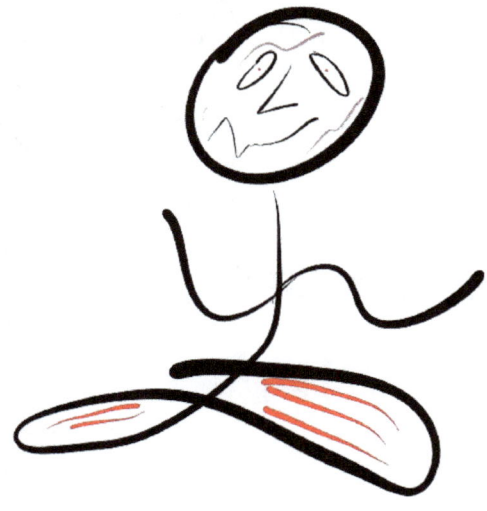

why are you looking at me?

CXXIII

my heart is broken—
i put it back together
with scotch tape and glue—

CXXIV

the sun is hanging
on to yesterday's blue sky
but it will not last—

CXXV

darkness always comes
at the end of every day
but the light returns—

CXXVI

love, hate, life and death
life is a merry-go-round
here we go again—

CXXVII

light evaporates
darkness covers everything
i just closed my eyes—

CXXVIII

tortured souls align
when broken hearts break free from
soul crushing despair—

CXXIX

death is a hunter
tracking my every move
my life fades away—

CXXX

when you closed your eyes
i became invisible
i just disappeared—

CXXXI

life passes us by
every day we move farther
from who we once were—

CXXXII

god wears disguises
but i can see through them all
god is a monster—

CXXXIII

many years ago
a man died upon a cross
trying to get home—

CXXXIV

you always return
when darkness overtakes me
interjecting pain—

CXXXV

the holy spirit
a cunning apparition
giving up the ghost—

CXXXVI

internal anger—
exploding deep within me
external danger—

CXXXVII

let your light shine through
eradicate the darkness
take over the night—

CXXXVIII

you never knew me
nor did i ever know you
we were never new—

CXXXIX

a cross erected
another christ crucified
he gave up the ghost—

CXL

language is an art
tongue-tied and misunderstood
a cunning linguist—

CXLI

you cut me with words
and make your apologies
as if you mean it—

CXLII

die on a cross and
walk through the resurrection
alone—all alone—

CXLIII

i grew up with god
he's my abusive father
but now i am free—

CXLIV

i thought you loved me
but i never thought you should
even when you did—

CXLV

standing on the edge
heaven and hell collide below
god is still a monster—

CXLVI

god—the monster king
demanding obedience
from all creation—

when I was a child, I spoke as a child, I understood as a child, I thought as a child; but when I became a man, I put away childish things. (*1 Corinthians 13:14*)

CXLVII

standing in shadows
darkness encompasses me
light can not escape—

CXLVIII

only god can stand
like a dog begging for bones
in his own temple—

CXLIX

the sun hanging on
to the day slipping away
can't stop the darkness—

CL

you found me again
staring at my reflection
as if it would change—

Life is the farce which everyone has to perform. — Arthur Rimbaud

CLI

standing before you
my heart is broken again
but you can't fix it—

CLII

you never saw me
but i was there the whole time
standing next to you—

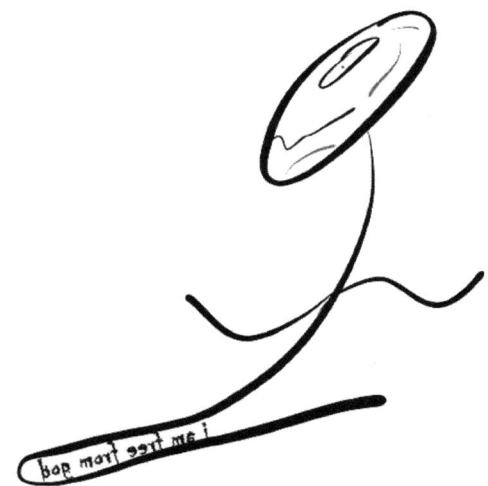

CLIII

another morning—
sun shinning through my window
as day breaks my soul—

CLIV

life has beat me down
until i became a shell
of the man i was—

All that we see or seem is but a dream within a dream — Edgar Allan Poe

CLV

my heart beats your name
and your heart beats me to death
love is bleeding out—

CLVI

time passes us by
yesterday has gone away
never seen again—

CLVII

death is there waiting
patiently like a stalker
moving through darkness—

CLVIII

today has ended
now we live for tomorrow
better days ahead—

CLIX

the pain was too much
i lived in my broken heart
alone—forsaken

CLX

i misunderstood
the meaning of life and death
but you always knew—

my god, my god, why hast thou forsaken me?

CLXI

satan is watching
from heaven disguised as god
it's always been so—

CLXII

time to start over
yesterday's a disaster
i'd rather forget—

CLXIII

i can not escape
the black hole surrounding me
my light has faded—

CLXIV

you tried to love me
but i was unloveable
i always have been—

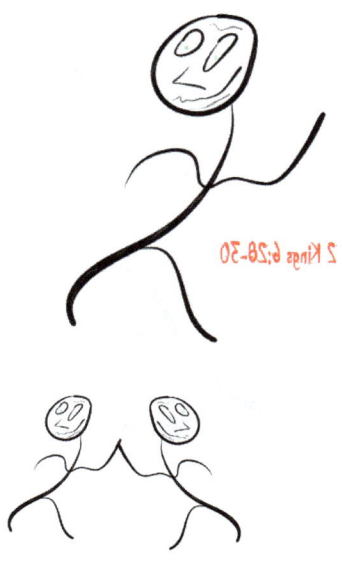

CLXV

bright lights—big city
skylines are lining the sky
night falls and day breaks—

CLXVI

son of lucifer
disastrous days ahead
for the fallen one—

CLXVII

please understand that
i'm not writing this for you
it's only for me—

CLXVIII

i'm a fake poet
trying to be the real thing
this book is my proof—

it is finished

Shadows & Light

Index of First Lines

angels in heaven **27**
another easter **6**
another easter— **37**
another morning **8**
another morning— **77**
another sunrise **32**
baptism by fire **60**
beneath the dark sky **37**
bright lights—big city **83**
a christ crucified **57**
cigarette burning **9**
a cross erected **70**
crucified again **31**
darkness all around **22**
darkness always comes **63**
the darkness of night **12**
death is a hunter **65**
death is there waiting **79**
the devil in me **12**
the devil's my friend **13**
die on a cross and **71**
a dying god-man **38**
every single day **59**
explosions in space **28**
the first day of spring **5**
five seven and five **50**
god and/or his son **21**
god is a demon **53**
god is a drifter **52**
god is defeated **26**
a god-man dying **47**

god's face in the sky **2**
god sits in heaven **24**
god—the monster king **73**
god wears disguises **66**
the greener the grass **22**
hearts that are broken **58**
heaven and hell are **14**
heaven lost its light **25**
heaven's reflection **43**
here i stand again **49**
here we go again **55**
the holy spirit **68**
i am not dead yet **4**
i can not escape **82**
i could never see **29**
i grew up with god **72**
if love were a war **60**
i'll never love you **51**
i'm a fake poet **84**
i'm dreaming of you **55**
i'm going to hell **47**
i misunderstood **80**
i'm living in hell **32**
in autumns' moonlight **3**
index of first lines **85**
in eternal light **44**
in pornography **5**
in space there's no sound **26**
in stillness we find **36**
internal anger **57**
internal anger— **68**
in the sky above— **29**
i thought you loved me **72**

ivy covered trees **50**
jesus and his whore **13**
jesus never could **52**
language is an art **70**
last night i saw you **39**
let your light shine through **69**
life and death collide **3**
life and death evolve **41**
life has beat me down **77**
life is a movie **20**
life passes us by **66**
light evaporates **64**
lightning cracks the sky **35**
like a razor blade **51**
look into my eyes **10**
losing the battle **61**
lost found lost again **49**
love—a symphony **36**
love, hate, life and death **63**
love is a demon **2**
love is a rocket **21**
love is the chorus **20**
love leaves no traces **27**
many years ago **67**
mary magdalene **16**
messiah or christ— **38**
my chest is empty **40**
my heart beats your name **78**
my heart has faded **56**
my heart is broken **18**
my heart is broken— **62**
my heart is shattered **17**
my heart skipped a beat **48**

my life has ended **19**
my mind is scary **44**
my nightmare's ended **58**
nature is a beast **48**
no one can hear you **41**
now i'm just a ghost **61**
now my heart's broken **40**
on lake washington **8**
only god can stand **74**
the pain was too much **80**
the path of the wind **10**
please understand that **84**
reading the bible **33**
recycle your words **54**
sacrificial lamb **42**
satan in disguise **25**
satan is watching **81**
she fucking hates me **4**
silently i wept **16**
sitting in heaven **54**
the sky is still blue **35**
sometimes i can't breathe **18**
sometimes life is kind **11**
son of lucifer **83**
souls locked in a war **46**
space—a solitude **42**
spring, autumn, winter **11**
standing before you **76**
standing in shadows **74**
standing on the edge **73**
stars fall and stars die **46**
stars fall from the sky **19**
the sun disappeared **45**

the sun hanging on **75**
the sun is hanging **62**
the sun is setting **45**
the sun is shining **43**
the sun says goodnight **56**
there is an echo **7**
this demon i see **17**
this is a haiku **30**
thunderstorms outside **30**
time is standing still **28**
time passes us by **78**
time to start over **81**
today has ended **79**
today is tonight **6**
today's a new day **14**
tortured souls align **64**
a total eclipse **24**
a tree standing tall **23**
two butterflies dance **9**
two butterflies dance— **23**
two conflicting views **33**
a voice in my head **1**
the war is over **34**
the war is over— **39**
we disappoint god **53**
we stand in darkness **1**
when i see this road **15**
when you closed your eyes **65**
a wooden cross stands **59**
years are passing by **7**
yesterday i fell **15**
yesterday is gone **31**
you always return **67**

you cut me with words **71**
you entered the room **34**
you found me again **75**
you never knew me **69**
you never saw me **76**
you tried to love me **82**

ghost riders
in the sky

Thank you Melissa
For letting me
Use your art
For the cover
Of this book—

Shadows & Light
Haiku/Senryū

Laughton J. Collins, Jr.

Shadows & Light

About the Author

Laughton J. Collins, Jr. was born in the 20th century but currently lives in the 21st century. He is originally from Georgia—currently living somewhere in the Pacific Northwest—in and/or around the Seattle area—He occasionally writes and publishes.

Also by Laughton J. Collins, Jr.

ghost riders in the sky and other lines

say goodnight to
—the ghost riders in the sky
in shadows & light

Find Me Online

Review/Feedback

Social Media

ghost riders on Amazon

Amazon Author Page

ghost riders sample

Author's Den

Profile Card

My Website

Links to Buy ghost riders

Requiem Press

Goodreads